MW01078888

Rio Grande
Through the Rockies

MIKE DANNEMAN

KALMBACH
BOOKS

Printed in the United States of America

02 03 04 05 06 07 08 09 10 11   10 9 8 7 6 5 4 3 2 1

Visit our website at
http://kalmbachbooks.com
Secure online ordering available

Publisher's Cataloging-in-Publication
Provided by Quality Books, Inc.

Danneman, Mike, 1963-
    Rio Grande through the Rockies / Mike Danneman. —
1st ed.
        p. cm.
        Includes index.
        ISBN: 0-89024-365-4

    1. Denver and Rio Grand Railroad Company—Pictorial
works. 2. Denver and Rio Grande Railroad Company—
History. 3. Denver and Rio Grande Western Railroad
Company—Pictorial works. 4. Denver and Rio Grande
Western Railroad Company—History. 5. Railroads—West
(U.S.)—Pictorial works. I. Title.

HE2791.D44238 2002   385'.0978
                                QBI02-200617

Art director: Kristi Ludwig
Book design: Kory Beavers

Cover photo: Rio Grande 1703 West is about to plunge into the 6.2-mile darkness of the Moffat Tunnel in August 1950. The huge curtain and blowers will come in handy to clear the tunnel of smoke once the train clears the West Portal. Photo by W. R. Breg, Jr.

The author would like to thank John Templeton, Rob McGonigal, and Mark Hemphill for their diligent proofreading efforts.

Contents

A Brief History of the Rio Grande

The central element of the Rio Grande is, of course, the Rocky Mountains, that vast barrier to transcontinental transportation that reaches its ultimate heights in Colorado. The Rio Grande crossed the Rockies several times; its standard gauge main lines crossed them twice. Any book on the Rio Grande must deal with the Rocky Mountains, and this book makes them its focus.

The Denver & Rio Grande—its originally incorporated name, on October 27, 1870 (the "Western" was added after several reorganizations and mergers)—was the creation of an unusually ambitious man, William Jackson Palmer. A veteran officer of the Civil War, Palmer had both engineering and construction experience, directing to completion the Kansas Pacific Railway from Kansas City to Denver. Palmer envisioned a north-south railroad that cut across the grain of the transcontinentals at the eastern base of the Rockies, feeding traffic to them. Palmer projected his line from Denver south to Santa Fe and eventually Mexico City.

The first spike was driven into a roughly hewn tie (3-foot or "narrow" gauge) on July 28, 1871, and by October 21 of the same year the railroad was completed to Colorado Springs. By 1876, Palmer's construction gangs, proceeding in fits and starts because financing was difficult, had extended the railroad nearly to the southern border of Colorado. The next step would be to climb over Raton Pass, the only feasible gateway into New Mexico. The Atchison, Topeka & Santa Fe, however, had designs on the same pass, and in a midnight raid took control of the pass and frustrated Palmer's southern ambitions.

It was an event that forever changed the Rio Grande, and probably for the better. Enormous precious metal discoveries in the Colorado Rockies brought huge investments to open mines, and mines needed railroads. But again only one suitable route into the rugged mountains was available, the Royal Gorge of the Arkansas

River west of Pueblo. Moreover, the gorge is so narrow in its depths that room is only available for one railroad. Both the Rio Grande and the Santa Fe lusted after the gorge, for the Arkansas River led directly to Leadville, then the greatest bonanza camp in the U.S. The "Royal Gorge War" ended with the Rio Grande owning the gorge, and the way was open to Leadville and dozens more bonanza camps.

From 1870 on, construction proceeded at a feverish pace. Utah at the same time had its own bumper crop of mineral strikes, so Palmer assembled another railroad to serve them, the Rio Grande Western. Observing that mineral traffic could move both ways between mines, mills, and smelters, Palmer connected the two lines in the middle, completing a narrow gauge main line from Denver to Salt Lake City on May 21, 1883.

On November 14, 1890, the Denver-Salt Lake City main line became standard gauge, though it was still too circuitous and expensive to operate to be considered a serious transcontinental competitor. In the 1920s and 1930s, considerable money was invested to straighten curves, ease grades, and improve the track structure.

As the twentieth century dawned a new threat stirred: the Denver, Northwestern & Pacific, projected to build a new main line from Denver due west to Salt Lake City, and perhaps onwards to the Pacific Coast. The DNW&P was like Palmer's Rio Grande the creation of an ambitious man, David Moffat; yet unlike Palmer, Moffat convinced almost no one that his new railroad would be a money-maker. Moffat's railroad expended most of his fortune clawing through the difficult canyons west of Denver and ran out of cash at Steamboat Springs, well short of his goal. That left the Moffat a dead-end branch line into the northwestern Colorado wilderness until the 1920s, when Denver businessmen, knowing that Denver needed more water in order to grow, cleverly coupled a water tunnel and railroad tunnel into one plan, and convinced voters in Denver and along the route of the Moffat Road to fund it with public bonds. The rail tunnel, opened in 1928, cut the Moffat Road's operating expenses, yet still it was a branch line to nowhere: that is, unless a 34-mile connection was built down the Colorado River from Orestod to Dotsero. The Dotsero Cutoff was completed in 1934, control of the Moffat Road was purchased by the Rio Grande (it was fully merged in 1947), and the Rio Grande could begin to challenge the Union Pacific and the Santa Fe for transcontinental freight and passenger traffic.

But that was then, this is now. The Rio Grande's route through the Rockies would never be the equal of the Union Pacific and Santa Fe's routes, which skirt the West's most rugged mountains. Regulation ended in 1980, and, other than coal, traffic on the Rio Grande has largely vanished. Denver businessman Philip Anschutz purchased the Rio Grande in 1983, merged it with the Southern Pacific in 1988, and sold the SP to the Union Pacific in 1997. The Rio Grande itself is back to being what it was in the 1880s: a collection of branch lines originating mineral traffic that happen to connect in the middle.

Yet this does not take away from the splendor of the Rio Grande, perhaps the most spectacular railroad ever. It certainly lived up to its motto: Through the Rockies, not around them!

Denver & Rio Grande Western

Main Line — Rio Grande — THRU THE ROCKIES

Rio Grande Locomotives

A railroad with big mountain crossings is bound to have big locomotives, and lots of them. In the steam era and in the diesel, the Rio Grande was always exceptional.

Yet even big railroads start small. Because the Rio Grande began as a narrow gauge, and until the 1920s its track structure was extremely light, it was fairly late to adopt the heavy steam locomotive.

If one was to characterize the railroad at the turn of the century, big power was 2-8-0s for freight and 4-6-0s for passenger. Not until 1910 did it order articulateds, eight small 2-6-6-2s, numbered 1050-1057, for helper service. Its first really large engines were 16 compound 2-8-8-2s, numbered 1060-1075, also initially for helper service. Both classes persisted in secondary assignments through World War II, renumbered in the 3300 and 3400 series, respectively.

Unlike most roads the D&RGW never purchased large numbers of Mikados or Pacifics—it preferred bigger power—having only one class of each type. These came in 1912-13: 14 2-8-2s numbered 1200-1213, and six 4-6-2s numbered 1001-1006 (later 800-805), assigned to fast freight and passenger, respectively. Another anomaly were its ten huge 2-10-2s, purchased in 1916. Initially the railroad intended these for mainline drag freight service, but with the poor track structure that then existed in Colorado they were soon reassigned to Utah, spending their entire career hauling coal over Soldier Summit. Later renumbered in the 1250 series, they were very successful in this job, lasting until the early 1950s.

Truly modern power arrived in the early 1920s as the railroad underwent complete reconstruction. For through freight service, the D&RGW purchased 30 4-8-2s numbered 1501-1530. These locomotives had the largest boiler ever secured to 4-8-2 running gear, at an astounding 96 inches in diameter. For helper service, also in 1923, came ten large compound 2-8-8-2s from Alco. Numbered 3500-3509,

▲ Dirt and grime sully 2-8-2 1209 at Salida, Colo., in March 1943. Too light for drag freight service, the 1200-series Mikados were utility engines useful for secondary passenger trains and in fast-freight helper service. Photo by H. K. Vollrath.

they worked their entire career in helper service on Soldier Summit.

The biggest and best of Rio Grande's steam was clearly its 20 3600-series simple articulateds. They were the world's most powerful locomotives when the first ten were delivered in 1927. They were used in mainline drag freight until diesels arrived in numbers, and in helper service until steam's end in 1956.

To speed up passenger trains on the steep mountain grades, the Rio Grande in 1926 bought ten very large three-cylinder 4-8-2s, numbered 1600-1609. Expensive to maintain, they would have all been scrapped by the early 1940s had World War II not intervened.

Much better were the 14 1700-series 4-8-4s purchased in 1929. Heavy and relatively low-drivered at 70 inches, they were highly successful in passenger service and later in fast freight. The final passenger locomotives purchased new were five 4-8-4s from Baldwin in 1937, in the 1800 series. Built to the latest design, they had 73-inch drivers and roller bearings. Their boilers had problems with cracks, however, and they did not last as long as the smaller 1700 series.

The last new steam engines purchased by the Rio Grande were its 15 3700-series 4-6-6-4s, ten arriving in 1938 and five more in 1942. These powerful locomotives were mostly used for fast freight between

Grand Junction and Salt Lake City.

The lessons learned from Electro-Motive Division's FT demonstrator were not lost on the D&RGW: it wanted as many as it could get. The first FTs arrived in 1941-42, greatly helping the Rio Grande to cope with wartime traffic. When it could not get more, the Rio Grande had no choice but to purchase two elderly 2-6-6-2s and 15 2-8-8-2s from the Norfolk & Western, along with four heavy, small-drivered 4-8-2s that the N&W found less than ideal. These were supplemented by six new 4-6-6-4s diverted from a 1945 Union Pacific order, leased from the War Production Board. The lease was dropped after the war,

▲ (Left) Four ex-Norfolk & Western 4-8-2s helped out with war traffic, but were all off the roster by 1948 because of high maintenance costs. The 1551 is dead at Burnham Shop in Denver in January 1948. Photo by H. K. Vollrath.

▲ (Right) Outstanding in dual service were the 1700 series 4-8-4s. The 1702 is at Denver on March 2, 1940. Photo by R. H. Kindig.

(Left) Some of Rio Grande's 3400-series compound 2-8-8-2s were heavily modified to increase performance and decrease maintenance costs. None of these ending up looking quite alike. The 3404, coaled and watered, is ready to dispatch westward from Helper, Utah, on June 11, 1947. Photo by R. H. Kindig.

(Right) The 1800-class 4-8-4s were purchased for the Rio Grande's premier trains. The 1800 displays its elegant lines at the north throat of Denver Union Station on August 31, 1940. Photo by R. H. Kindig.

and they went to the Clinchfield.

Merger of the Denver & Salt Lake into Rio Grande in 1947 brought a collection of elderly locomotives to the roster. Many were never renumbered and retired at once, though some of the Moffat Road's 2-6-6-0s lasted until 1952. The mainline steam era ended in 1956, with 3600-series 2-8-8-2s working out of Tabernash in helper service to the West Portal of Moffat Tunnel. The final steam runs were in December, 1956, by heavy 2-8-0s from Alamosa on the Creede Branch.

The diesel era

During the early 1940s Rio Grande purchased dozens of diesel-electric switchers from builders GE, Alco, Baldwin, FM, and EMD to replace steam in yards. Not until the first FTs were delivered in 1942 was there serious competition between steam and diesel for the mainline freight trains. A total of 48 FTs in four-unit A-B-B-A sets were bought from 1942 to 1944.

In 1947, in anticipation of the new *California Zephyr*, Rio Grande purchased two A-B-A sets of Alco PAs. These engines were the premier power for the *CZ* in the early years but were relegated to secondary trains in the 1950s because of high maintenance costs and unreliability. The PAs were initially used on the *Exposition Flyer* until the full *CZ* sets were delivered in 1949.

One dozen F3s were purchased in 1946, in three A-B-B-A sets. The B units were equipped with steam generators for passenger service.

These units powered the *California Zephyr* and *Prospector* until retired.

From 1948 to 1952, Rio Grande acquired 86 F7s and six F9s for freight service, all in four-unit A-B-B-A sets. F9A 5771 and F9Bs 5762 and 5763 would soldier on after Amtrak on the *Rio Grande Zephyr*, until Amtrak began operating over the Rio Grande in 1983.

The road-switcher type ended the dominance of the "covered wagon." Fourteen GP7s brought on line in 1950 and 1952, and 24 GP9s bought in two batches in 1955-56, also ended the steam era forever on Rio Grande standard gauge lines. For heavy-duty service Rio Grande purchased five SD7s in 1953 and ten SD9s in 1957. The SDs were normally assigned to branchline mineral service, mostly in Utah,

whereas the GP9s and GP7s were used in every type of service. Since four F7s did not have quite enough horsepower to meet the Rio Grande's operating plan, frequently a single GP7 or GP9 was spliced into the middle of an A-B-B-A F-unit consist.

By the late 1950s the Rio Grande, like most railroads, was looking to replace its first-generation diesels, and it wanted more horsepower in one package to cut maintenance costs. To do this the Rio Grande looked overseas, agreeing with the Southern Pacific to purchase and import six 4,000 hp diesel-hydraulic prototype units from Krauss-Maffei of Germany in 1959. The Rio Grande's three, 4001-4003, were shipped in late 1961. These locomotives were not the

success that was hoped for—maintenance costs were breathtaking and availability and reliability underwhelming. No more K-Ms for the Rio Grande! Instead, when EMD announced the new 2,250 hp GP30, Rio Grande was one of the first in line. FTs went to the builder in trade. The GP30s were the first road units on Rio Grande delivered in plain black with "Grande gold" striping on the ends, rather than the expensive orange, silver, and black scheme used on the F units and the K-Ms. The simple and inexpensive black-and-gold scheme was previously used only on switchers. The first GP30s arrived in 1962, and an additional order received in 1963 put the total at 28.

The follow-up locomotive from EMD was the 2,500 hp GP35. Rio

Grande bought 22 of these locomotives. The complex electrical system necessary to achieve the extra horsepower proved expensive and troublesome, and by 1972 all were relegated to B-unit status, and stored during traffic downturns.

EMD's new 645-powered series with A.C. main generators became the mainstay of Rio Grande's locomotive fleet, from their introduction in 1965 until the end of the Rio Grande with merger. For fast freight, the Rio Grande preferred the 3000 hp GP40. The 43 GP40s that arrived in 1966 to 1971, along with 37 later GP40-2s and second-hand GP40s from Conrail, were good, reliable locomotives. For drag freight, 26 3600 hp SD45s arrived in 1967-68. Some of these were the first units to receive the

▲ (Left) One of the ex-Norfolk & Western Y2s, No. 3551 (formerly N&W 1722), is parked at Burnham Shops in Denver on May 30, 1948. Photo by R. H. Kindig.

▲ (Right) Powerful, easy on track for their size, and without excessive maintenance expense, Rio Grande's 3600-series 2-8-8-2s were probably the best heavy steam locomotives the Rio Grande ever bought. No. 3609 coals at Grand Junction on May 31, 1941. Photo by R. H. Kindig.

▲ (Left) Rio Grande EMD F3 5534 is dressed in the simplified single-stripe scheme. This scheme appeared sooner on passenger power than on freight. Louis A. Marre collection.

▲ (Right) The unique lines of Krauss-Maffei ML-4000 are seen at Denver in July 1963. Louis A. Marre collection.

new large Rio Grande logo, the better to promote a new unit coal-train (joint with Union Pacific) between Kaiser Steel's Sunnyside Mine in Utah, and its steel mill at Fontana, Calif.

The new backbone of modern Rio Grande fleet was the SD40T-2. First arriving in 1974, these units were ordered in large numbers for the rapidly expanding coal business. Known as "tunnel motors" for their cooling system, the SD40T-2s were even more successful than the GP40s. All were equipped by Rio Grande with Positive Traction Control, an aftermarket wheel-rail adhesion system, to improve tractive effort on poor rail conditions with maximum tonnage.

◄ Second-generation GP30
No. 3008 rests between runs.
Photo by Hillard N. Proctor.

◄ No. 5324 is a 3,600 h.p.
EMD SD45 from 1968. Louis A.
Marre collection.

Moffat Tunnel Route

▶ While the Rio Grande was one of the owners of Denver Union Station, the Moffat Road was not—it has its own station several blocks to the north in the warehouse district. With inclusion in the D&RGW, Moffat Road passenger trains began using Union Station: Rio Grande 1701 arrives off the Moffat under the umbrella sheds of Denver Union Station. Photo by Joseph Schick.

Denver financier David Moffat was frustrated. Booted from the presidency of the Denver & Rio Grande by a board that saw no interest in building new routes, he sat in his office at the First National Bank of Denver and contemplated building a main line directly to the west, through the formidable Front Range of the Rocky Mountains. But no one would join him in what they saw as a fools' errand: Moffat's dream, to succeed, would fight for traffic with Edward H. Harriman's mighty Union Pacific-Southern Pacific combination, not to mention the Rio Grande itself.

No matter. Moffat incorporated the standard gauge Denver, North-western & Pacific Railway, and began building west from Denver in 1902. Two major problems confronted the Moffat Road's engineers. The first was to find a moderate grade that would take the railroad into the mountains, and the second was to build a tunnel under the main range itself, as no pass of sufficiently low altitude across the range existed.

The first problem was relatively easy to solve. Moffat's engineers used sidehill construction, loops, and a substantial amount of tunneling to project a 2 percent grade right to the base of the main range. The second problem needed money Moffat didn't have, so he gambled

on a temporary line across Rollins Pass in the hopes that traffic would come in such volume that he could build the tunnel out of cash flow, or by borrowing.

This was not to be. In the midst of an economic boom where railroads were borrowing tens of millions at low rates to build new lines and improve existing lines, no one thought enough of Moffat's scheme to lend it money, and operating costs on the temporary line over Rollins Pass were staggering. Moffat ran out of cash with his railroad ending quite literally in the middle of nowhere, with the hoped-for traffic growing far slower than anticipated.

When Moffat died in 1911, his railroad was bankrupt, ending at Steamboat Springs. Other Denver investors scraped enough money together to extend the Moffat Road—now reorganized as the Denver & Salt Lake–onward to Craig, Colo., but no farther.

With the completion of the 6.2-mile Moffat Tunnel using public money in 1928, and the completion of the Dotsero Cut-off to connect the Moffat to the Rio Grande main line in 1934, part of Moffat's ambition was realized: Denver now lay on a direct transcontinental route. The original route over Rollins Pass was abandoned, with no tears shed by the railroaders who had to operate it. But the rest of the Moffat Road from Orestod to Craig was a branch line, and the air-line route to Salt Lake City remains today just a dream.

As it turned out, this branch line to Craig would have great value. Vast coal fields in northwestern Colorado, of minor economic importance in Moffat's day, became valuable when the demand for electricity rose in the 1960s. The Moffat began generating three or more unit trains of coal daily, and what was once a fairly inconsequential branch line was rebuilt to mainline standards, with big rail and Centralized Traffic Control.

Today, as part of the Union Pacific, the Moffat Tunnel Route today is dispatched from UP headquarters in Omaha. While the through freight business has largely been rerouted to the UP main line through Wyoming, the Moffat is still valuable as an originating coal route, both for mines on its own line as well as mines on the North Fork Branch east of Grand Junction. It's still the route of a passenger train, too, Amtrak's daily *California Zephyr*. David Moffat might not like to see the heirs of his one-time archrival E. H. Harriman running his railroad, but the huge tonnage operated today, compared to the old days of Mallets struggling over Corona Pass, would probably console him.

◄ The *California Zephyr* leaves Denver Union Station in July 1952 with mixed Alco and EMD power. A through train from Chicago to Oakland, Calif., operated by the Chicago, Burlington & Quincy, Rio Grande, and Western Pacific, the *CZ* was widely regarded as the most successful pure "cruise train" of the classic era. Photo by Donald Sims.

◄◄ Pacific 801 and Mikado 1210 double-head out of Denver with train No. 5, the *Exposition Flyer,* on June 17, 1939. At this time, 4-8-2s and 4-8-4s were not allowed on the Moffat Tunnel Route because of light rail and weight restrictions on bridges, so passenger trains used 4-6-2s or 2-8-2s instead. Photo by R. H. Kindig.

◄ Mikado 1205 leaves the control of the Denver Union Terminal operator, passing beneath the signal bridge at the north end of Denver Union Terminal. It will enter the Moffat Road proper at Prospect. Photo by Marsh F. Beall.

◄◄ Dusk falls upon Denver Union Station on February 26, 1953. Power for the evening's westbound No. 7, the *Prospector,* is to the left. This well-regarded night train to Salt Lake City ran out of passengers in the 1960s, unable to compete with airlines for the business traveler. Photo by Wallace W. Abbey.

◄ Rio Grande No. 10, the *Yampa Valley,* threads through Union Pacific's 20th Street Yard at right and the Burlington's coach yard at left to arrive at Denver Union Station in early 1965. The *Yampa Valley* was a daytime coach-and-mail train running to Craig, Colo. Photo by George H. Drury.

▲ A short train No. 7, the *Prospector,* leaves Denver on the evening of June 6, 1942. Here in the floodplain of Clear Creek the main line was nearly flat, but in a few miles the 2 percent ramp to the Moffat Tunnel will begin. Northwest Denver no longer looks like this, of course! Photo by Jackson C. Thode.

▶ On a chilly winter morning in 1940, the *Exposition Flyer* heads west near Ralston, so named for Ralston Creek. Rio Grande 4-8-4 1804 moves the nine-car train along at a brisk 50 mph. Ralston no longer exists as a station, and today this area is mostly light industrial. Photo by R. H. Kindig.

◄◄ (Top) Dynamic brakes whining, an A-B-B-A FT set leads an eastward freight down the 2 percent just west of Leyden on January 14, 1945. Photo by Otto C. Perry.

◄◄ (Bottom) Rio Grande's original two-car Budd-built *Prospector* didn't last long — November 17, 1941, to July 5, 1942 — so action photos of first iteration of this overnight Denver-Salt Lake train are rare. No. 7 motors up the 2 percent west of Leyden on the evening of May 14, 1942. Photo by Otto C. Perry.

◄ A double-headed 14-car westbound *Exposition Flyer* storms through the cut just east of Arena (now Rocky) on February 22, 1946. Road engine 1705 is helped by 4-8-2 1513. The 1513 will cut off at East Portal and return to Denver. Photo by R. W. Michael.

◄ New FT set 541, purchased in 1942, climbs westward approaching Arena. With the consolidation of CTC offices beginning in the early 1950s many station names were changed to avoid conflict: Arena became Rocky in 1952. Photo by John W. Maxwell.

▲ A Ski Train with black-and-yellow F7s heads west in the deep cut east of Rocky in 1952. The name Rocky comes from the Rocky Flats, a broad alluvial plain at the base of the Rockies strewn with loose rocks. Photo by R. H. Kindig.

Having just met a westward passenger train at Arena, an eastward drag pulls out of the siding behind compound 2-8-8-2 3408. The westward passenger has already advanced beyond the west switch and can be seen in the distance on the approach to the Big Ten loop. Photo by F. L. Jaques.

◀◀ D&SL 4-6-0 300 leads train No. 1 into the Big Ten loop on January 28, 1940. Above the train is the hamlet of Fireclay, where clay was mined for firebrick. Clay siding, renamed as such in 1939, extends along the hillside in the background. Photo by R. H. Kindig.

◀ A little later the same morning, the westbound *Ute*—short for Utah Express—pounds upgrade into the Big Ten curve west of Arena. The *Ute* was a daily fast freight out of Denver for Salt Lake City in the morning, built from local traffic and traffic received from the Burlington in Denver. The 3401 will help the train to the Moffat Tunnel. Photo by R. H. Kindig.

◄◄ Rio Grande 4-6-0 789 leads the last train No. 8, the *Prospector*, down from Coal Creek into Denver on July 4, 1942. Discontinued for the war, the *Prospector* was reinstituted as a diesel-powered train in 1946. The dirt road in this view will become today's Blue Mountain Drive. Photo by R. H. Kindig.

◄ FT set 542 crosses Coal Creek and the road overpass east of Tunnel 1 with a 55-car westbound freight. Pushing hard on the rear is helper 4-8-2 1513. A long, curved steel trestle once carried the D&SL over Coal Creek at this location; it was too light for engines like the 1513 and replaced with this fill and culvert. Both photos by J. W. Maxwell on March 14, 1942.

▲ Westward train No. 9 stops at the Coal Creek water tank on June 16, 1948. At this flat spot in the 2 percent ruling grade, trains could take water and restart without great difficulty. Photo by Ross B. Grenard.

◂ Train No. 9 with 4-6-2 No. 805 storms away from its water stop at Coal Creek on January 10, 1948, and onto the 2 percent. In a few seconds it will curve through Tunnel 1, around another curve, and its engineer will look at the signal at the east switch of Plainview. Photo by Ralph E. Hallock.

◄ Eastbound train No. 10 exits Tunnel 1 east of Plain and heads downgrade toward Coal Creek on October 24, 1950. Photo by Herbert O'Hanlon.

▲ The siding at Plainview — now just "Plain" — extends through Rainbow Cut and right to the east portal of Tunnel 2. A 16-car eastward freight behind a former Moffat Road 2-6-6-0 is about to enter Rainbow Cut on February 11, 1949. Photo by R. H. Kindig.

◂ On April 30, 1939, at 9:18 a.m., a 44-car *Ute* steams out of Tunnel 2 behind double-headed 2-8-8-2s. Both 3404 and 3410 have auxiliary water cars, a common practice on the Moffat Road to reduce water stops. Photo by R. H. Kindig.

◂ Westward tonnage received from the Burlington climbs through the tunnels west of Plainview in April 1964. In the distance the train disappears into Tunnel 3. Check out the new Fords! Photo by Richard Steinheimer.

▲ In April 1964, train No. 17, the *California Zephyr,* leaves the plains of Colorado behind as it climbs through Tunnel 3 west of aptly named Plainview. Photo by Richard Steinheimer.

▶ Train No. 9 approaches Tunnel 3 west of Plainview behind 4-6-2 801 on April 26, 1950. The upthrust sandstone of the Flatirons provides a splendid backdrop for the little train. Photo by Henry R. Griffiths, Jr.

▶ On December 7, 1941, at 10:17 a.m., the 3401 drifts downgrade at Tunnel 6 west of Plainview with a 46-car freight. Already the U.S. is at war, though it's doubtful either train crew or photographer knew it at the moment this photo was taken. Photo by John W. Maxwell.

▶ Rio Grande 2-8-0 1146 helps 2-8-8-2 3406 with 27 cars up the 2 percent grade between Crags and Crescent at milepost 29, on July 12, 1938. The heavy 2-8-0 would be big power on a prairie railroad, but here it's pretty small. Photo by Henry R. Griffiths, Jr.

▶ Train 17, the westbound *California Zephyr,* enters Tunnel 17 east of Crescent on July 29, 1961. The four-unit F3 set was delivered in a scheme of black with yellow stripes and now wears the bright scheme of orange, silver, and black stripes. Photo by R. H. Kindig.

▶▶ The heavyweight *Exposition Flyer* works west in the upper reaches of South Boulder Canyon about 2 miles east of Pinecliff behind 4-8-2 1803 on July 5, 1941. Here the railroad is several hundred feet above South Boulder Creek, but the creek is rising at a faster rate than the railroad, and at Pinecliff the two come together. Photo by Henry R. Griffiths, Jr.

▶ Train No. 5, the *Panoramic*, threads through short Tunnel 28 east of Pinecliff in August 1935. A through train to Salt Lake City, the *Panoramic* was fairly typical of Rio Grande first-class trains prior to World War II: pleasant but not spectacular in its appointments. Photo by R. H. Kindig.

▲ and ▶ Rio Grande F5 5561 leads a 77-car, 3975-ton train No. 77 through the remains of Tunnel 28 in April 1951, with 4-8-4 1701 helping on the rear. Tunnel 28 was daylighted because of constant rock falls and ground pressure; the rock above it was highly weathered and fractured. Two photos by R. H. Kindig.

◄◄ (Far left) The *California Zephyr* twists through South Boulder Canyon east of Pinecliff in the summer of 1951. One of the As of the Alco PA-PB-PA set has been replaced today by an EMD F3B. The PAs wear a short-lived silver-and-orange scheme. Photo by W. H. Mitchell.

◄◄ (Center) The *Yampa Valley* curves through the site of Tunnel 28. An Alco PA/EMD F3 leads the three-car train on its trip to Craig. Photo by Jim Shaughnessy.

◄ The last run of the *California Zephyr* ascends South Boulder Canyon just east of Pinecliff on March 21, 1970. Passenger service will not end, however; the *Rio Grande Zephyr* will continue with tri-weekly service. Photo by William H. McKenzie.

▲ Huge 2-8-8-2 3615 storms across South Boulder Creek just west of Tunnel 29 at Pinecliff with the second section of a 32-car train 41. It is 9:27 a.m. on July 5, 1941. This timber trestle was later replaced with a steel through-plate-girder. Photo by John W. Maxwell.

▶ A former Denver & Salt Lake 2-6-6-0 waits in the siding short of the grade crossing at Pinecliff, meeting a late-running westbound *Exposition Flyer* with brand-new Alco PA-PBs. Note the water column. Photo by W. H. Mitchell.

▶ Rio Grande 1704 and 1801 get a drink from the waterplug at Pinecliff on June 22, 1943. Practically all westward trains on the Moffat needed a helper between Denver and the Moffat Tunnel. Photo by Robert A. LeMassena.

▶▶ Helper 1516, a 4-8-2, has wyed at East Portal after helping a westward freight. It's just met another westward train at Cliff. The signaling system on the Moffat was upgraded to Centralized Traffic Control during World War II. Photo by W. H. Mitchell.

▶ A set of new FTs on First 78 rolls eastward on the approach to Pinecliff on June 1, 1944. Summer cabins in the background were and still are popular with Denver residents. Photographer R. H. Kindig was disappointed that morning, hoping to find one of Rio Grande's 3600-series 2-8-8-2s on the point of this train.

◀ The *Ute* pounds upgrade west of Pinecliff on May 26, 1940. D&RGW 3413 helps road engine and 3606, both 2-8-8-2s. Even with the help, the 48 cars are only moving at 25 mph. Photo by J. W. Maxwell.

▶ Denver & Salt Lake train No. 1, the day train to Craig, rounds a sharp curve in Rollins Canyon just east of Rollinsville. The D&SL's low-drivered 2-8-0s were ideal for its route, but not much good for heavier trains. Few lasted long after the merger with the D&RGW. Photo by Ragsdale.

◄ The bottles rattle in the Pirate's Den at Rollinsville with the passing of a westward freight with five F7s. Photo from Louis A. Marre collection.

▲ A troop train storms westward just east of Tolland on May 16, 1943. Photo by Robert McKell.

◀ The bulbous contours of a German-built Krauss-Maffei are framed by a caboose cupola window on October 11, 1963. The K-Ms were testing in helper service between Denver and East Portal in this instance on symbol freight PBX. Photo by R. P. Parsons.

◀ Krauss-Maffei 4001 shoves hard on the caboose of westbound PBX on the train's climb to the Moffat Tunnel on October 11, 1963. Photo by R. P. Parsons.

▶ Big Rio Grande 2-8-8-2 3602, heading up a westward freight, takes the siding at Tolland to meet the eastbound *Exposition Flyer*. Photo by W. C. Stearns.

▶▶ On July 7, 1941, Denver & Salt Lake 122 on train No. 1 approaches East Portal at 15 mph. The bridge crosses South Boulder Creek and the county road. Photo by H. R. Griffiths.

▶ Rio Grande FTs lead an east-ward freight at East Portal in October 1947. The twin lines through the trees in the distance are surveyor's lines, cut during the construction of the Moffat Tunnel. Photo by L. O. Merrill.

◀ Westbound symbol freight CD with GP30s 3021, 3022, 3023, and 3024 waits at East Portal for an eastward with GP30s 3025, 3026, 3027, and 3028. The GP30s are brand-new on this date—May 4, 1963—and their nice numerical order won't last long. Photo by Bruce R. Meyer.

▲ At one time both portals of the Moffat Tunnel were equipped with high-pressure car-washing sprayers to clean windows in preparation for the splendid views ahead. This is the view out of East Portal in 1949. Photo by W. H. Mitchell.

◄◄ In January 1968, a westbound freight bursts into daylight at the West Portal after 6.2 miles of darkness in the Moffat Tunnel. Photo by Robert J. Yanosey.

◄ Two F7s and an FT bring a train toward the west portal of the Moffat Tunnel at Winter Park on August 1955. Three more units push on the rear of the train. The Winter Park ski area is at left; today, its buildings, ski lifts, and parking lots dominate this scene. Photo by Parker Hayden.

◄ The local from Craig approaches the West Portal of the Moffat Tunnel at Winter Park in September 1949. The portal can be seen directly over the rear of the last car. Note the very poor track. Photo by A. C. Kalmbach.

▲ On December 27, 1947, a four-unit set of EMD F3s grinds up the grade to the Moffat Tunnel at Winter Park with 48 cars, at 20 mph. Steam helpers were common for eastward drag freights. Photo by Ross Grenard.

▸ Regal PA 6003 leads the west-bound *Yampa Valley* leaving Granby on April 5, 1964. Both heavy-weight and lightweight equipment were used on this train, depending on what was available. Photo by George H. Drury.

▸▸ The Continental Divide is seen from the first car of an eastbound freight in the early 1960s. This is the range originally crossed at Rollins Pass; today's route lies below almost all of the heavy snow zone. Photo by R. P. Parsons.

▶ Snow lurks in crevices on the Front Range well into the summer. Down along the Colorado River it's warm and sunny. Eighty-five cars pulled by a matching set of F7s head west out of Granby in 1959. Photo by D. J. Davidson.

◀ A new set of four FTs on a westward freight passes beneath the U.S. 40 overpass just east of Hot Sulphur Springs. Photo by the Denver & Rio Grande Western Railroad Co.

▲ Train No. 10 tiptoes through the rocky confines of Byer's Canyon just west of Hot Sulphur Springs on September 5, 1949. Photo by R. H. Kindig.

◄ A fireman's view out of the PA on train 10 at Flat, as a westward freight hustles by on the main line in October 1964. Photo by John Gruber.

◄ New Year's Eve of 1966 finds both *Yampa Valleys* meeting at Radium. Train No. 10 is in charge of Alco PA 6001 and is seen from the cab of 6013, on the point of No. 9. Photo by Steve Patterson.

◀ An eastward mainline freight from Grand Junction pulls out of Orestod behind 4-8-2 1505. The Craig Branch departs the main line just out of the frame at left and begins climbing out of the river canyon. Photo by G. L. Campbell.

▲ The *Yampa Valley Mail* has climbed high above the Colorado River on its way to Toponas Divide. Here it is west of Volcano at the entrance to Egeria Canyon. The main line is in the bottom of the valley in the far distance. Photo by R. H. Kindig.

◄ Bond as a station or town did not exist until the construction of the Dotsero Cutoff in the early 1930s. Its coaling tower and enginehouse are seen from the dome-observation of train No. 18, the *California Zephyr,* in February 1950. The smoke in the background is from train No. 9 heading out of town up on the Craig branch. Photo by Willard V. Anderson.

◄ Train No. 10 leaves Steamboat Springs eastbound on July 16, 1949. The brick depot was a Moffat standard; similar depots were built at Hayden and Craig. Photo by Robert Wietzke.

◀◀ *California Zephyrs* meet in Glenwood Canyon shortly after inauguration in 1949. This was a frequent meeting place, unless one train was late. CB&Q photo, Donald Ashton.

◀ From the cab of eastbound No. 18, the *California Zephyrs* meet in Glenwood Canyon at Grizzly. Steep, slow, and with short sidings, Glenwood Canyon was a daily bottleneck that confounded unwary dispatchers. Photo by Al Rung.

◄ Two miles east of Glenwood Springs, train 17, the California Zephyr, passes through splendid Glenwood Canyon with a spiffy A-B-A set of Grande PAs. Photo by Bob Borcherding in August 1952.

▼ Five F7s with a westbound freight pass through beautiful Glenwood Canyon on April 25, 1965. David P. Morgan Library collection.

▲ D&RGW 3607, one of Rio
Grande's huge Alco 2-8-8-2s, is
shown arriving at Glenwood Springs
with a 51-car "Ute" freight on April
21, 1940. Photo by R. H. Kindig.

Tennessee Pass

▶ Train No. 1, the *Scenic Limited,* charges into the Royal Gorge west of Canon City. The normal consist is swollen by extra sleepers in this war-torn year of 1942. Photo by William Moedinger.

The Rio Grande's Tennessee Pass line has a history fit for a Hollywood movie. General William Jackson Palmer began his narrow gauge railroad, the Denver & Rio Grande Railway, at Denver and headed south for the border of Mexico. He didn't get far. Raton Pass was already occupied by the Santa Fe, so he shifted his vision toward the rich mining towns of western Colorado.

Santa Fe had the same idea. Both railroads began construction west of Pueblo toward the narrow defiles of the Royal Gorge. There was a catch. The Arkansas River at the bottom of Royal Gorge allowed only enough room for one railroad.

The famous "Royal Gorge War" ensued between the two railroads, some of it even in the courts. Rio Grande lost Raton Pass but was victorious in the Royal Gorge. These decisions would ultimately give the railway a future in transcontinental freight and passenger traffic.

The Rio Grande narrow gauge headed west along the Arkansas, reached Leadville in 1880, and was built over Tennessee Pass to Glenwood Springs by 1887. The line over Tennessee Pass was essentially a narrow gauge branch.

At about this time, the standard gauge Colorado Midland was beginning to make itself known in these regions. This put great competitive strain on the narrow gauge.

The Midland never faced the problems of transloading shipments that the D&RG did. To counter, the D&RG and the CM agreed to build a joint standard gauge railroad from Rifle to Grand Junction to connect with the Rio Grande Western. Of coarse, the Rio Grande Junction Railway worked to the D&RG's advantage in the long run. Also at this time, RGW undertook the massive regauging and rebuilding of its own narrow gauge line across Utah.

Narrow gauge would remain a rich part of the Rio Grande for much of its life, but not over Tennessee Pass. A new standard gauge line was built over the pass between Malta and Pando with the

▸ Eastbound train 2, the *Royal Gorge,* passes through its namesake below the famous suspension bridge in March 1964. Photo by Richard Steinheimer.

conversion of standard gauge from Pueblo to Grand Junction in 1890. The rails through the Royal Gorge (between Pueblo and Salida) remained dual gauge (both standard and narrow gauge three-rail) for several more years.

This route, combined with the D&RG subsidiary Rio Grande Western in Utah, gave the new Denver & Rio Grande Western the route it was looking for. Sure, the main line between Denver, Pueblo, and Salt Lake City was circuitous. But the D&RGW was in the transcontinental railroad business.

For the first part of the twentieth century, Rio Grande did what it could for traffic, competing with much superior railroads like Union Pacific for transcontinental traffic. World War I caused the line to boom, and modernization was undertaken between 1924 and 1930. New rail was laid on the entire route, and the first CTC (Centralized Traffic Control) west of the Mississippi was located between Tennessee Pass and Deen Tunnel.

A second route for the Rio Grande became reality with the construction of the Moffat Tunnel and the Dotsero Cutoff. The Moffat became the preferred through route, but Tennessee Pass still was an important line to the railroads in the Kansas City gateway.

The Tennessee Pass line was famous for its steep 3 percent grade from the helper base of Minturn to the summit of Tennessee Pass, at 10,212 feet the highest mainline crossing in the United States. Millions of tons of coal, ore, and other merchandise have flowed over the scenic divide. The rails over the pass are rusty and silent today, but the hope is that someday the modern Union Pacific will again route traffic over the scenic splendor that is Tennessee Pass.

▶ The westbound *Scenic Limited* is shown in the depths of rugged Royal Gorge in June 1937. Engine 773, a 4-6-0 Alco, leads road engine 1710, which is a Baldwin 4-8-4. Photo by M. C. Poor.

◄ Passengers aboard the *Royal Gorge* are enjoying the customary ten-minute stop at the foot of Hanging Bridge in the train's name-sake canyon. The suspension bridge overhead hangs between the canyon walls 1,053 feet above the Arkansas River. Photo by Denver & Rio Grande Western Railroad Co.

◄ An eastbound freight, led by a brand-new set of GP9s, pauses to change crews at Salida on December 16, 1955. Photo by Jim Shaughnessy.

▲ The *California Zephyr* gets dusted with cinders by the Salida switcher in a rare detour over the Royal Gorge Route because of a washout on the Moffat Tunnel Route. Note the three-rail tracks; the Monarch branch out of Salida was still narrow gauge on June 18, 1951. Photo by Bob Borcherding.

◄◄ Just west of Princeton, a westbound freight is about to cross the Arkansas River. The river and the railroad have shared the right-of-way through the mountains since leaving Pueblo. Photo by LeRoy Wilkie.

◄ Train No. 61 crosses the Arkansas River west of Yale (now called Balltown on the present highway), led by class engine 3600 on October 22, 1939. Photo by R. H. Kindig

◄ The 1517 on train 2-36 runs a clean stack as she rolls downgrade, eastbound at Keeldar, between Tennessee Pass and Malta. Photo at 4:28 p.m. on July 3, 1941, by John W. Maxwell.

◀ Rio Grande 3613 is about to enter the west portal of Tennessee Pass Tunnel in October 1946. Photo by R. H. Kindig.

◀ Train 61, the California Fast Freight, is leaving the Tennessee Pass station, in April 1938, crossing the Continental Divide at an elevation of 10,212 feet. The able 2-8-8-2 3606 will keep the train in check down the steep 3 percent grade to Minturn. Photo by R. H. Kindig.

▲ Train 1-36 is about a mile short of the top of Tennessee Pass at Mitchell at 8:15 a.m. on October 5, 1947. Road engine 1553 is assisted by helpers 3555 and 3601 with the heavy 30-car train. Photo by Ralph E. Hallock.

▲ A unique view of a double-headed diesel/steam tandem with the eastbound *Royal Gorge* at Mitchell. Photo by Harry N. B. Hospers.

◀ A set of F3s grinds upgrade at Mitchell in October 1947. Two steam helpers provide the necessary assistance up the 3 percent grade. Photo by L. O. Merrill.

◀ and ▲ The end of steam on the Tennessee Pass didn't end the show of machines versus gravity. This 47-car eastbound has three GP30s and a GP35 on the point, and four Fs and two Geeps midtrain at Mitchell. Both photos on September 11, 1969, by David W. Salter.

► A Civilian Conservation Corps special is seen climbing the Pass near Mitchell on March 24, 1940. The 3615 and 1526 smoke up the Colorado sky in this heroic portrait. Photo by R. H. Kindig.

► Rio Grande 3601 pounds up-grade at 10 mph, emerging from the Deen Tunnel, east of Pando, with 58 cars and two helpers. The U.S. Army's 10th Mtn. Division's Camp Hale (used in both winter and summer) is seen in the background of this photo, taken on March 30, 1946. Photo by R. H. Kindig.

◀◀ and ◀ Rio Grande 1517 emerges from Eagle River Canyon west of Redcliff with second No. 36 on July 3, 1941. The 50-car train is assisted upgrade by helper engines 3404 and 3414, both 2-8-8-2s. Photos by J. W. Maxwell.

► Four GP30s and a GP35 lead No. 54 at Belden, in the depths of Eagle River Canyon, just west of Redcliff. Two F7s helpers also push on the caboose of the hotshot. Photo by William H. McKenzie.

◄ Huge 2-8-8-2 3600 is seen climbing the west slope of Tennessee Pass at Rex, just east of Minturn. Helping the 3600 on August 15, 1954, with the 42-car train are equally huge sisters 3607 and 3615. The echoes in the Eagle River Canyon on this day must have been awesome! Photo by R. H. Kindig.

▲ Locomotives 3617 and 1800 lead train No. 2, the *Royal Gorge*, out of Minturn in September 1949. A trip up Tennessee Pass, aspens in blazing color, led by a 3600; what could be better? Photo by Ross B. Grenard.

◀ A triple-headed *Royal Gorge* leaves Minturn in the smoke on August 30, 1947. Eighteen cars make up the consist of No. 2 today. Photo by C. L. Carson.

▲ The eastbound *Scenic Limited* waits at Minturn for a new crew (head-end) and the customary air test and inspection of the train. It's the summer of '38, and this train often ran in two or three sections! Photo by R. H. Kindig.

◄◄ Rio Grande F7s 5611-5612-5613-5614 on an eastbound freight are pulling into Minturn Yard on February 19, 1966. Helper units 5684 and 5691 sit to the left. Photo by Ed Fulcomer.

◄ There's no denying which route Rio Grande 3606 east is plying on this day. The 58-car train is shown crossing the Eagle River on July 3, 1941. Photo by H. R. Griffiths.

Rio Grande's Passenger Trains

Throughout the history of the Rio Grande, passenger service was part of the railroad. Perhaps it was the amazing scenery that was on every traveler's itinerary, or the remoteness of many of the communities that were on line. This scenic beauty and remoteness gave the railroad much local passenger business. The Rio Grande was the "Scenic Line of the World," and passenger trains were the way to see it.

The *Royal Gorge* (trains 1-2) ran between Denver and Salt Lake via the Royal Gorge and Tennessee Pass. This train was the successor to the *Scenic Limited*, which ran over the same route prior to June 2,

1946. The *Royal Gorge* was combined with the *Prospector* between Grand Junction and Salt Lake after 1950. On December 6, 1964, the *Royal Gorge* was cut back to Salida, and the train was discontinued on July 27, 1967.

Trains 3 and 4, the *Colorado Eagle,* were actually Missouri Pacific trains run by Rio Grande from Pueblo to Denver. The trains were discontinued on May 16, 1966.

The *Panoramic* (trains 5-6) was a train that took advantage of the new Moffat Tunnel and Dotsero Cutoff and was operated starting on July 17, 1934. This train was replaced by the startup of the *Exposition Flyer* on June 11, 1939, with the same numbers. This train in

turn became the *California Zephyr* (trains 17-18).

The *Prospector* (trains 7-8) was an overnight favorite for business travelers between Denver and Salt Lake. Dieselization produced a pair of ill-fated vest-pocket two-car Budd streamliners on November 17, 1941. After fewer than nine months, on July 5, 1942, the *Prospector* was dropped from the timetable, mostly because of the war. The train was brought back with conventional equipment on October 1, 1945. Extra equipment was purchased from C&O via Pullman and arrived in 1950 to give the train new life. But losses to the bottom line caught up to the train, and the *Prospector* was

▶ This is the view from aboard train No. 1, the *Royal Gorge,* as it approaches the Hanging Bridge in the depth of the gorge. The two Alcos have the four-car train well at hand on April 15, 1959. Photo by Jim Scribbins.

discontinued on May 28, 1967.

Trains 19-20 were the *Mountaineer,* an overnight train that handled head-end and local business between Denver and Grand Junction on the same route as the *Prospector.* This train ran on to Montrose, Colo. The last run of the train was on October 24, 1959, at which time the *Prospector* gained the head-end business.

Rio Grande trains 9-10 had a long and interesting history. Origi-nally the trains were operated by the Denver & Salt Lake from Denver to Craig. With the merger with the D&RGW, the trains became 9-10, local service to Craig. The last run for the train came on December 31, 1950. Then on September 5, 1954, the *Yampa Valley Mail* was back. The "Mail" in the name was officially dropped when the Post Office ended mail service on the train in November 1963. Over the years, many people still referred to the train as the *Yampa Valley Mail,* even when it wasn't officially used. The train gained justifiable fame toward the end of its life as the final duty for Rio Grande's PAs. The train was discontinued on April 7, 1968.

Probably the most famous Rio Grande-operated train was the *California Zephyr* (17-18). This premier Budd domeliner was operated with partners Burlington and Western Pacific between Chicago and San Francisco. The first run was on

March 20, 1949, and it became one of the most celebrated trains in the country. Speed was not of the essence, and the train was scheduled through most of the spectacular scenery in daylight for the pleasure of the passengers. All good things must come to an end, and the *CZ* died a controversial death on March 22, 1970. Or did it?

The Rio Grande, maverick that it is, decided to not join Amtrak, and ran its own little train between Denver and Salt Lake. The *Rio Grande Zephyr*, also trains 17-18, ran back and forth on a tri-weekly schedule. But never on Wednesday. People could experience the beautiful Colorado and Utah scenery from the classic Budd-built dome cars to the end, which unfortunately came in April 24, 1983. The splendid scenery of the crossing of the Rockies can still be seen today from the lounge windows of Amtrak's *California Zephyr* (trains 5-6).

Rio Grande also had a long-standing history with winter enthusiasts of Denver and operated a Ski Train to the west slopes of Colorado. The first Ski Train was run in 1936 to Hot Sulphur Springs; the destination changed to Winter Park when that ski area was developed in 1946. The Ski Train has run every year since. If you want to catch a glimpse of a Grande gold and silver passenger train, check out the Ski Train!

⬆ (Left) Rio Grande 1210 is seen drifting out of Tunnel 12 with a nine-car train No. 6, the *Panoramic*. A few weeds and not a lot of ballast can be seen on the roadbed this July 12, 1938. Photo by R. H. Kindig.

⬆ (Right) Train No. 6, the eastbound *Exposition Flyer*, is high above South Boulder Creek on July 5, 1941. Photo by Henry R. Griffiths, Jr.

▲ This is the last run of train 10 at Tunnel 29, east of Pinecliff, on December 31, 1950. Of course trains 9-10, the *Yampa Valley Mail*, are brought back again on September 5, 1954, and are photographically famous as the final stompin' grounds for Rio Grande's PAs. Photo by Otto C. Perry.

▶ The *California Zephyr* climbs the front range on the morning of June 30, 1949, between Tunnels 2 and 3. The PA-PB-PA set is seen in the short-lived scheme of solid silver with a "Grande gold" nose. Photo by Ralph E. Hallock.

▶▶ Beginning in 1964, trains 7 and 8, the *Prospector,* frequently carried a car or two of TOFC to help out the bottom line. But to no avail—the train was discontinued in 1967. The eastbound No. 6 is shown here at East Rocky in April 1964. Photo by Richard Steinheimer.

▶ Rio Grande PA 6013 descends the front range just after leaving Tunnel 1, bound for Denver with train 10, the *Yampa Valley,* on August 13, 1966. Only two of the four PAs Rio Grande owned ever received the single-stripe paint scheme. Photo by J. W. Swanberg.

▶▶ (Opposite) The classy dome-observation "Silver Sky" brings up the rear end of train No. 17, the *Rio Grande Zephyr,* at Plainview on June 17, 1978. Photo by John R. Taibi.

The Modern Rio Grande

The classic era for many railroads ended in 1980 with the advent of deregulation—along with the end of most railroad-operated passenger trains and the coming of Amtrak in 1971. The Rio Grande did things a little differently. It decided not to join Amtrak in 1971 and ran a tri-weekly passenger train between Denver and Salt Lake instead, the *Rio Grande Zephyr*. Without sleepers and the long-distance aura of the *California Zephyr*, at first the *RGZ* seemed a bit of a letdown. But as time went on, it developed a following all its own. The classic original equipment of 1949 soldiered on, pulled by three F9s, the last cab

units on the Rio Grande. The 5771 has to be one of the most photographed diesel locomotives ever.

The Rio Grande also ran a Ski Train every winter, made up in part of eight classic ex-Northern Pacific heavyweight coaches. Running since 1936, the Ski Trains to the west slope from Denver have become an annual institution and still run today.

But the real thing that made the Rio Grande unique long after other railroads seemed homogenized was the spectacular scenery and the big trains. In fact, after the Southern Pacific merger, traffic on the Rio Grande surged to levels the railroad didn't even have during World War II. Tennessee Pass was a particular

thrill, because it had both trains in numbers and trains in weight, with taconite trains heading west and coal trains east.

The "modern" Rio Grande may not seem to belong in a book devoted to classic trains; but if you look at some photos from this time, I think you'll agree that those years were golden too.

▲ A Moffat coal drag, with Rio Grande's unique tunnel motors (EMD SD40T-2), meets train No. 83 at Yarmony in June 1976. Photo by Richard Loveman.

▶ The Ski Train climbs through Tunnel 29 east of Pinecliff in January 1973. The car behind the two locomotives is a steam generator, made from the tender of a Rio Grande 3700 series 4-6-6-4. Photo by Mel Patrick.

◀ Dirt-filled hoppers were put on the inside of Big Ten Curve between Rocky and Clay to act as a windbreak. They kept the ferocious gusts that blow off the Front Range from taking trains with it. Several derailments occurred (especially with high-profile piggyback cars) until the windbreak was installed in late 1971. Photo by Ray Kenley.

▲ Westbound hotshot No. 87 snakes through the 10-degree curves of Coal Creek Canyon on April 9, 1977. The railroad crosses the mouth of the canyon between Clay and Plain on the climb to the Moffat Tunnel. Photo by Richard Loveman.

The Rio Grande Lines Today

▶ The Rio Grande Ski Train, with its "new" ex-Amtrak F40PHs painted in Rio Grande colors, is a great way to get a feel for the now-departed Rio Grande. Photo by Mike Danneman.

There's not all that much left of the Rio Grande today other than its track. A dirty, weathered freight car rolls by once in a while. Several bridges still have the famous "flying Rio Grande" logo on it. And the right-of-way still has those familiar white No Trespassing signs, albeit with the D&RGW initials painted out.

Unfortunately, Tennessee Pass no longer has any train traffic. But the Royal Gorge does, thanks to tourist trains and rock trains. And on the Moffat and Soldier Summit, UP and trackage rights tenants Burlington Northern Santa Fe and Utah Railway keep the rails shiny.

But the biggest thing that keeps the mystique of the Rio Grande alive is the wonderful scenery, which is just as good now as it ever was.

Want to experience the Rio Grande? Go trackside on the Union Pacific's Moffat Tunnel Subdivision on a Saturday or Sunday morning during the winter. The Ski Train can give you a wonderful glimpse of some Grande gold and silver! And the train runs on summer weekends too.

Rio Grande Diesel Locomotives

Series	Type	Builder	Year(s)	Series	Type	Builder	Year(s)
38-43	44-ton	GE	1941-42	5100-5113	GP7	EMD	1950-52
66-74	VO660	Baldwin	1941	5200-5204	RS3	Alco	1951
100[1]	NW2	EMC	1941	5300-5304	SD7	EMD	1953
101-119	S2	Alco	1941-44	5305-5314	SD9	EMD	1957
120-123	H10-44	FM	1948	5315-5340	SD45	EMD	1967-68
130-139	SW1200	EMD	1964-65	5341-5413	SD40T-2	EMD	1974-80
140-149	SW1000	EMD	1966-68	5501-5517	SD50	EMD	1984
150-152	H15-44	FM	1948	5401-5514[5]	FT	EMD	1942-44
3001-3028	GP30	EMD	1962-63	5521-5544[6]	F3	EMD	1946
3029-3050	GP35	EMD	1964-65	5561-5764[7]	F7	EMD	1948-52
3051-3093	GP40	EMD	1966-71	5762-5763	F9B	EMD	1955
3094-3130	GP40-2	EMD	1972-83	5771-5774[8]	F9	EMD	1955
3131-3153[2]	GP40	EMD	1968	5901-5954[9]	GP9	EMD	1955-56
3154-3156[3]	GP60	EMD	1990	6001-6013[10]	PA1/PB1	Alco	1947
4001-4003[4]	ML-4000	K-M	1961				

Notes

[1]Originally numbered 7000, Rio Grande's first diesel
[2]Purchased from Conrail in 1983
[3]Last locomotives delivered in Rio Grande paint
[4]Built in West Germany by Krauss-Maffei
[5]Total of 48 units, in A-B-B-A sets
[6]Total of 12 units, in A-B-B-A sets
[7]Total of 86 units, in A-B-B-A sets, see notes below
[8]One four-unit A-B-B-A set
[9]Total of 24 units
[10]Total of 6 units

Note: Rio Grande had a peculiar way of numbering its cab units. The FT, F3, and early F7s were delivered in A-B-B-A sets with one three-digit number assigned to the entire set. When the realization set in that the units could be split up, a new numbering system was devised. A numeral 1, 2, 3, or 4 was simply added to the three-digit number of each unit of the consist. For example, the four-unit set of F3s numbered 552 became 5521, 5522, 5523, and 5524. Therefore, All Rio Grande F cab units end in the digit 1 or 4, and all boosters end in digits 2 or 3. GP9s for some reason were numbered in this same pattern, but the GP7s purchased earlier were not! The PAs were similar, only they were in A-B-A sets. They became 6001, 6002, 6003, and 6011, 6012, 6013. Also, the last two F7 sets were delivered in A-B-A sets, and the missing B-units were filled in with F9Bs in 1955. Also note that the only numbers used twice are 5401-04 and 5411-13, which were FTs, and later SD40T-2s; and 5501-5504 and 5511-5514, which were FTs, and later SD50s.

Modern Rio Grande Steam Locomotives

Series	Type	Builder	Year (s)	Series	Type	Builder	Year (s)
800-805[1]	4-6-2	Baldwin	1912	3300-3307[6]	2-6-6-2	Alco	1910
1200-1213	2-8-2	Baldwin	1912	3350-3351[7]	2-6-6-2	Alco	1942
1220-1229[2]	2-8-2	Lima	1915	3360-3375[8]	2-6-6-0	Alco	1909-16
1400-1409[3]	2-10-2	Alco	1916	3400-3415[9]	2-8-8-2	Alco	1913
1501-1530	4-8-2	Alco	1922-23	3500-3509	2-8-8-2	Alco	1923
1550-1553[4]	4-8-2		1945	3550-3564[10]	2-8-8-2	Baldwin	1943, 1945
1600-1609[5]	4-8-2	Alco	1926	3600-3619	2-8-8-2	Alco	1927, 1930
1700-1713	4-8-4	Baldwin	1929	3700-3714	4-6-6-4	Baldwin	1938, 1942
1800-1804	4-8-4	Baldwin	1937	3800-3805[11]	4-6-6-4	Alco	1943

Notes

[1]Former road numbers 1001-1006
[2]1220-1227 were built by Lima, 1228-1229 built by Alco/all were former D&SL 400-409
[3]Former road numbers 1250-1259
[4]Built at N&W Roanoke Shops
[5]World's heaviest 4-8-2s
[6]Former road numbers 1050-1057
[7]Ex. Norfolk & Western
[8]3360-3369 built 1909-1910 for DNW&P as 0-6-6-0s/all were former D&SL 200-216
[9]Former road numbers 1060-1075
[10]3550, 3556, 3558, 3559 built at N&W's Roanoke Shop
[11]Union Pacific specifications, diverted by War Production Board and leased

Note: Narrow gauge locomotives, and smaller standard gauge 0-6-0, 2-8-0, and 4-6-0 type engines not included in this roster. The following initials are: N&W—Norfolk & Western, DNW&P—Denver Northwestern & Pacific, D&SL—Denver & Salt Lake.

Rio Grande Passenger Trains, 1948

1	Denver to Grand Jct.	*Royal Gorge* (former *Scenic Limited*, renamed in 1946)
2	Grand Jct. to Denver	*Royal Gorge* (former *Scenic Limited*, renamed in 1946)
3	Denver to Pueblo	*Colorado Eagle* (contracted to run Denver-Pueblo for Missouri Pacific)
4	Pueblo to Denver	*Colorado Eagle* (contracted to run Pueblo-Denver for Missouri Pacific)
5	Denver to Salt Lake	*Exposition Flyer* (train becomes *California Zephyr* on March 22, 1949)
6	Salt Lake to Denver	*Exposition Flyer* (train becomes *California Zephyr* on March 22, 1949)
7	Denver to Salt Lake	*Prospector*
8	Salt Lake to Denver	*Prospector*
9	Denver to Craig	*Yampa Valley Mail* (local service)
10	Craig to Denver	*Yampa Valley Mail* (local service)
11	Marysvale to Salt Lake	(local service)
12	Salt Lake to Marysvale	(local service)
15	Denver to Alamosa	*Colorado & New Mexico Express* (local service, trains 15-115-215 run as combined)
16	Alamosa to Denver	*Colorado & New Mexico Express* (local service, trains 16-116-216 run as combined)
19	Denver to Montrose	*Mountaineer*
20	Montrose to Denver	*Mountaineer*
23	Denver to Craig	(local service, leaves Denver Monday, Wednesday, and Friday)
24	Craig to Denver	(local service, leaves Craig Tuesday, Thursday, and Saturday)
115	Pueblo to Alamosa	*Colorado & New Mexico Express* (local service, trains 16-116-216 run as combined)
116	Pueblo to Alamosa	*Colorado & New Mexico Express* (local service, trains 16-116-216 run as combined)
215	Alamosa to Durango	*San Juan* (narrow gauge)
216	Durango to Alamosa	*San Juan* (narrow gauge)
461	Durango to Silverton	*Silverton* (narrow gauge, Tuesday, Thursday, and Saturday during summer tourist season only
462	Silverton to Durango	*Silverton* (narrow gauge, Tuesday, Thursday, and Saturday during summer tourist season only

Note: All information from Rio Grande May 30, 1948, public timetable. Also note that train names *Yampa Valley Mail* or *Yampa Valley* for trains 9-10, *Colorado & New Mexico Express* for trains 15-115 and 16-116, and *San Juan* for 215-216 trains were not officially used in the timetable at this time. These trains were simply listed under "local service."

Rio Grande Passenger Trains, 1966

101	No. 1 Denver to Salida	*Royal Gorge*
102	No. 2 Salida to Denver	*Royal Gorge*
103	No. 3 Denver to Pueblo	*Colorado Eagle*
104	No. 4 Pueblo to Denver	*Colorado Eagle*
105	Extra Denver South	
106	Extra Pueblo North	
107	No. 7 Denver to Salt Lake	*Prospector*
108	No. 8 Salt Lake to Denver	*Prospector*
109	No. 9 Denver to Craig	*Yampa Valley*
110	No. 10 Craig to Denver	*Yampa Valley*
111	Ski Train Denver West	
112	Ski Train Tabernash East	
113	Open	
114	Open	
115	Open	
116	Open	
117	No. 17 Denver to Salt Lake	*California Zephyr*
118	No. 18 Salt Lake to Denver	*California Zephyr*

Note: The number 1 ahead of the train number was in line with the 1966 train renumbering in which the first number designated the "section" of the train run. For example, a second section of train number 2 would be 202

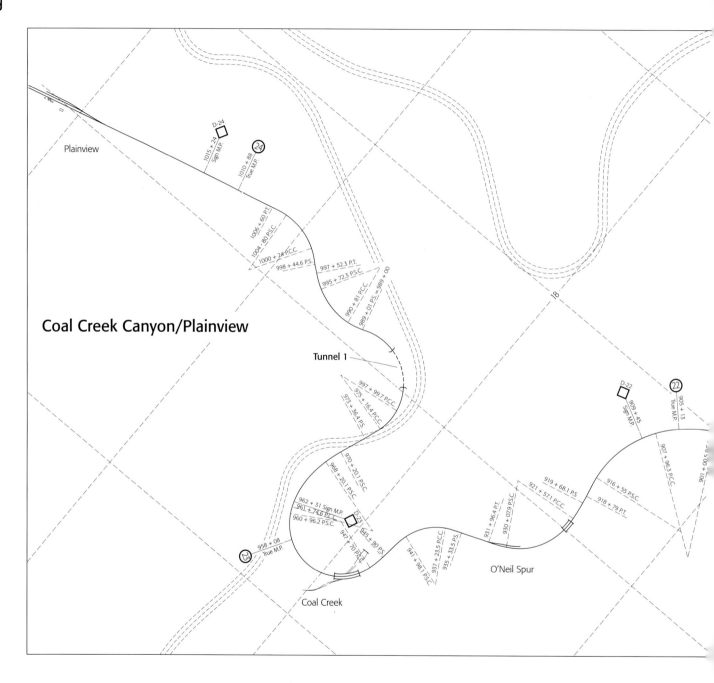

Coal Creek Canyon/Plainview

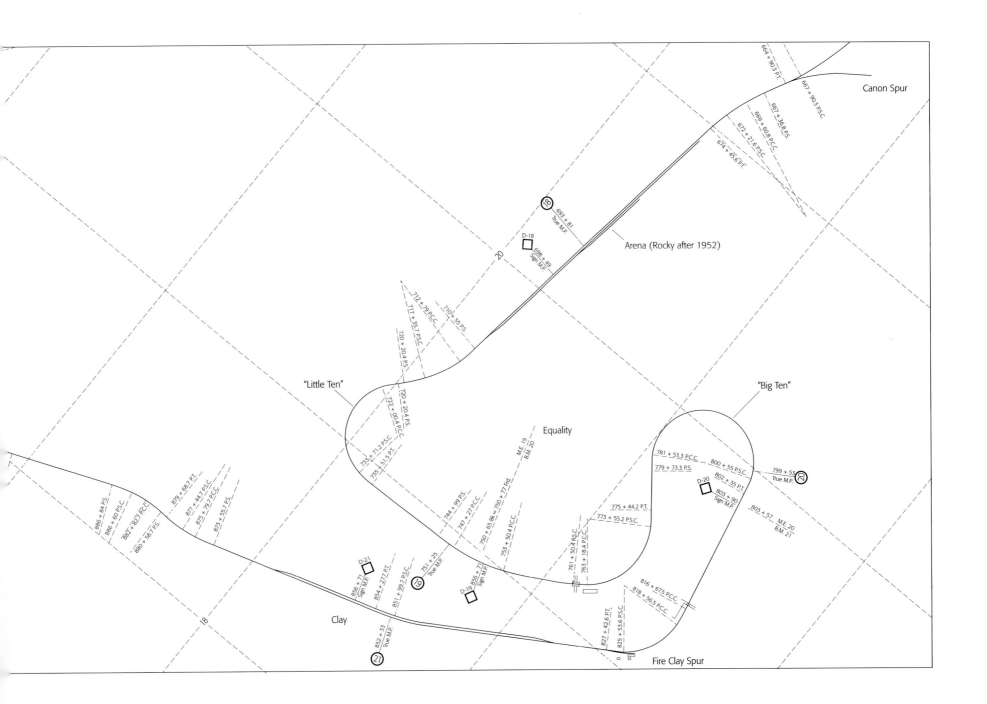

Canon Spur

664 + 90.3 P.T.
667 + 90.3 P.S.C.
667 + 36.8 P.S.
669 + 60.8 P.C.C.
672 + 21.6 P.S.C.
674 + 45.6 P.T.

Arena (Rocky after 1952)

⑱ 693 + 81 True M.P.

D-18
698 + 49 Sign M.P.

20

712 + 79 P.C.C.
712 + 35.7 P.S.C.
710 + 55 P.S.
720 + 20.4 P.S.

"Little Ten"

720 + 20.4 P.S.
722 + 00.4 P.C.C.

"Big Ten"

Equality

733 + 71.2 P.S.C.
733 + 51.5 P.T.
735 +

M.E. 19
B.M. 20

781 + 53.3 P.C.C.
779 + 73.3 P.S.
800 + 55 P.S.C.
802 + 35 P.T.

799 + 53 ⑳
True M.P.

D-20
803 + 90 Sign M.P.

803 + 57   M.E. 20
B.M. 21

744 + 99 P.S.
747 + 27 P.C.C.
750 + 65 B.M. = 750 + 71 Frd.
753 + 50.4 P.C.C.

775 + 44.2 P.T.
773 + 55.2 P.S.C.

761 + 50.3 P.S.C.
763 + 18.4 P.C.C.

886 + 84 P.S.
886 + 60 P.S.C.
882 + 82.7 P.C.C.
880 + 58.7 P.S.
879 + 68.7 P.T.
877 + 44.7 P.S.C.
875 + 79.7 P.C.C.
873 + 55.7 P.S.

816 + 675 P.C.C.
818 + 56.5 P.C.C.

D-21
856 + 71 Sign M.P.
854 + 277 P.T.
851 + 99.7 P.S.C.

751 + 25 ⑲
True M.P.

D-19
856 + 71 Sign M.P.

Clay

852 + 33 True M.P.

18

827 + 42.6 P.T.
825 + 53.6 P.S.C.

Fire Clay Spur

㉑

125

Tennessee Pass

1. Tunnel
2. Watchman's Shanty
3. Telltale
4. Banjo Semaphor Disc.
5. Block Limit Sign
6. Well House
7. Water Tank
8. House for Train Crew
9. Carbody use as Tool House
10. Shed
11. Car Inspector's House
12. Bunkhouse
13. Carbody
14. Pumphouse
15. Well
16. Carbody
17. Carbody
18. Depot
19. Stock Yards
20. Well House
21. Derail & Post
22. Derail
23. Derail Post
24. Trestle
25. Trestle

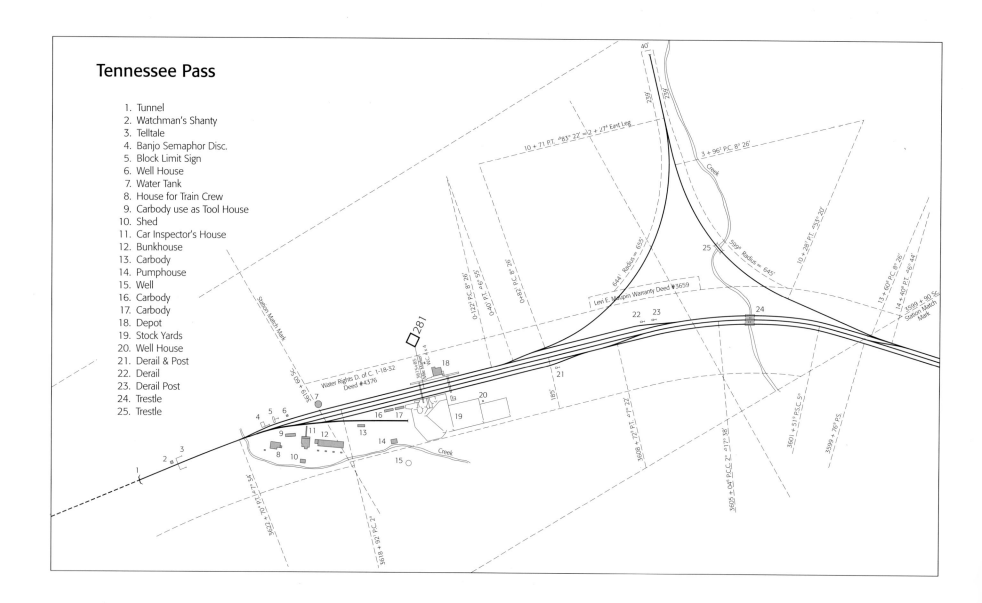

Index of Photographs

Photographers

Passenger trains